NOT SURE
WHO NEEDS
TO HEAR
THIS, BUT ...

NOT SURE WHO NEEDS TO HEAR THIS, BUT ...

Beautiful Reminders for the Soul

Willie Greene
Founder of WE THE URBAN

CLARKSON POTTER/PUBLISHERS
NEW YORK

May the journey back to yourself
be safe, gentle, and secure.

CONTENTS.

Chapter One

PEACE.

Through every experience you have in this life, turbulent or otherwise, a boundless space exists within you. It's a secret sanctuary we all carry, that we can all access. It may seem elusive at times, drowned out by the noise of anxiety, grief, and regret, but it's always there, patiently waiting for you to cherish its presence and make decisions that align with protecting it. This refuge is your inner peace.

Your inner peace should flow like a river, traveling forward despite the rocks and boulders that arise. Adapting and persisting, knowing that your journey is dictated not by obstacles but by your unwavering pursuit to transcend them. This endurance and resilience is not passivity; it's an understanding that peace is not something that demands an *escape* from the chaos of your life, but rather invites you to find serenity *within* the very heart of it. The moment you start acknowledging that peace is not an external place but an internal commitment to self-awareness and acceptance, you unlock the door to a life less anxious and more tranquil.

Even so, attaining inner peace can be a daunting quest, especially if you're someone like me, who feels *everything* deeply. However, I've learned that these qualities of sensitivity and peace have a unique relationship. In fact, they can exist in harmony. This sounds paradoxical; how can feeling every emotion intensely lead to inner peace? Well, it fuels your imagination and serves as a wellspring of creativity. It enhances your intuition and allows you to appreciate the beauty in the tiniest nuances of life. It makes you want to listen more, understand better, and empathize more deeply with others. You get the privilege of engaging with life, love, and connection in the most vivid, profound way. Your sensitivity can become a gift that empowers and protects you. It's a quality you should never shame yourself for having. With time, introspection, and a big helping of mindfulness, you can access inner peace in a space of sensitivity.

The pursuit of peace can also lead us to seek comfort in fleeting relationships, places, substances, and possessions. These are common traps we've all been caught in at some point, but the reality remains the same: peace built on external distractions is as fragile as a house of cards in a hurricane. Authentic peace can *only* be cultivated from within. It demands the hard work of confronting yourself and demolishing the walls you've constructed from your fears. It calls for the bravery to cease the war within yourself, to declare a truce between the parts of you in conflict, and to treat yourself with more kindness. When you make peace with your inner turmoil, your outer world begins to mirror this tranquility.

Throughout this process, your strength lies in identifying and amplifying the thoughts that serve your mind, body, spirit, and future. Let them be the architects of your day. Your mind's focus determines your reality—what you pay attention to, you give power to, so you must choose with fierce *intentionality*. Let the stillness of your inner peace, and the energy of unapologetically protecting it, be the compass that directs your thoughts. This is a conscious exercise of selecting, moment by moment, the thought patterns that lead you to a more peaceful existence. By channeling this mindfulness, peace becomes more than just a concept; it becomes a practice.

Envision each day as a fresh chance to refine this practice. Just like you might train for a marathon or learn a new language, cultivating peace is a skill. It means choosing not to snap in anger, taking a deep breath instead of taking a defensive stance, or finding that moment of gratitude on a tough day. It's the determination to persist after rejection, the relief in releasing long-held grievances, and the awareness that holding on to anger harms you more than anyone else.

Peace is your right, your responsibility, and your remedy. It is the brave decision to wake each morning and forgive. Forgive each day for its trials, forgive others for their faults, and most importantly, forgive yourself for your missteps. It's in this forgiveness that you free yourself, lifting all burdens and opening the gates to true inner calm.

Inner peace means respecting that not everything deserves your energy and granting yourself permission to walk away from fruitless conflicts. If something disturbs your peace, you have the right—and, indeed, the responsibility—to address it, to modify it, or to remove it altogether from your life. Sometimes, the most powerful armor is a smile and the decision to let go. Protect your peace like you would your dearest loved one.

True peace? It will always be a choice. It's a series of decisions you make every day. Sometimes it's the decision to release, other times the decision to hold on, but it's *always* the decision to reflect and grow. It's about accepting the unchangeable and finding your power in how you respond to it. With each decision, you step closer to accessing the calm you seek.

So, here's to the journey of accessing your well of inner peace, hand in hand with your sensitivity—a journey of introspection, understanding, and giving yourself the space to feel and the permission to heal. Continue to approach yourself with grace and move forward at a pace that honors your growth. Trust that with each action you take, you're gaining wisdom and finding your balance, navigating your way back to that serene sanctuary that is ever-present within you.

NINE WAYS TO ACCESS PEACE.

1.

PRACTICE RADICAL ACCEPTANCE.

Get in the habit of letting things simply be what they are. It's easier said than done, but that is why the art of *practice* is essential. Acceptance doesn't mean giving up or being passive. It means tapping into peace by responding to turbulence with greater resilience and adaptability. It means freeing your mind and nervous system from gainless struggles. It's understanding that draining your energy by worrying never improves the outcome. Embracing this truth is one of the most profound acts of self-love. Understand that life is unpredictable, and you can only control so much. The faster you accept these things, the faster you will transcend them.

2.

DISCONNECT TO RECONNECT.

You are not a robot. It is not natural for you to take in a ton of information at once, follow the minutia of thousands of people's daily lives, rely on "likes" to inform your worth, or expect yourself to be productive 24/7. The paradox of the digital age is that while it has connected us to the world, it has disconnected us from ourselves. This is especially true if, like most people in the modern world, your livelihood relies on using the internet in some capacity.

So, amid the whirlwind of your commitments and the cacophony of external demands, *pause*. Take a breath and tune in. Dedicate time each day to disconnect from it all. Try implementing screen-free mornings and evenings. Go outside at least once a day. Lean into your in-person connections. If you want peace, be more available to your real life.

The goal is to aim for a balanced use of technology that helps rather than hinders your well-being.

3.

FORGIVE YOURSELF.

If you are pursuing peace, forgiving yourself is a great place to start. You are not your mistakes. You have grown from the past versions of yourself. You are more than the situations you put yourself in that led to hard-learned lessons. You are a person who deserves grace at this moment, not shame. Sitting around punishing yourself for things you regret is the quickest way to steal your peace. The emotional liberation of forgiving yourself allows you the opportunity to grow, change, and become better. Give yourself that chance. You deserve more than being in a dark place, disappointed in yourself. Meet yourself with compassion and take back your power.

4.

BE MINDFUL.

Please give your overthinking mind a break. You'll be hard-pressed to find peace when you're not doing the inner work to get there. Instead of stressing about the future or dwelling on the past, take moments throughout the day to be present.

Focus on your breath, notice your surroundings, and remove unnecessary distractions. Set aside time each day for meditation, yoga, journaling, or reflection to observe your thoughts and emotions without judgment. Finding discipline in these practices will give you the gift of self-awareness, allowing you to challenge negative thought patterns, manage triggers, and respond to adversity with a calm, sound mind.

5.

PRACTICE GRATITUDE.

Practicing gratitude is the ultimate bridge to peace amid chaos. It might sound cliché, but it's life-changing. It's so easy to get caught up in the pursuit of more, constantly feeling behind and striving for what you don't have. In doing so, we often overlook the blessings surrounding us. The truth is that you always have enough, do enough, and *are* enough. *Always*. The transformative power of internalizing this idea cannot be understated. Take out a journal or take time to write down three things you feel grateful for every day. Remember, you won't find peace by bottling up your feelings, acquiring more possessions, or constantly moving the goalpost every time you reach an accomplishment. You can nurture a grateful heart by valuing your present abundance.

6.

FIND YOUR PEOPLE.

We all want to belong; it is a fundamental human need. Whether you're introverted or not, maintaining and finding connections you cherish is imperative for your mental health. This goes way beyond surface-level connections. It's about leaning on the people in your life who feel like your soulmates. People who cherish and uplift you with no ulterior motives or unfair conditions. People with whom you can be your authentic self and engage in meaningful conversations that help you both grow. For your peace, invest energy in these relationships. And if you haven't found them yet, keep searching. I promise you, they are out there.

7.

ASK FOR HELP.

You don't have to carry everything by yourself. There is no shame in getting help, and you don't have to be at your lowest to ask for it. Seeking professional support is a sign of strength, not weakness. It's telling yourself, "Hey, I love you. I respect you. I want to invest in your growth. You deserve to live a healthy, balanced life." There are myriad professionals trained to help you through your toughest moments, actively waiting to be there for you. Therapists, counselors, psychologists, and psychiatrists can provide invaluable guidance. And if the monetary costs keep you from getting help, there are online resources with more affordable or even free options for you. I'm sending you love on your journey toward mental wellness.

8.

SIMPLIFY
YOUR LIFE.

The state of your space reflects the state of your mind. They work together and influence each other. That feeling of peace you get when everything is clean and in its place is no coincidence. This is your reminder to declutter your physical space, your mind, and your time. Delete old messages and apps that don't serve your growth, turn off unnecessary notifications, set boundaries, clean out your closet, let go of objects that hold the weight of memories you don't need to hold on to, and reexamine who gets the privilege of experiencing your energy. Release it all. Embracing a minimal approach to life will always serve your peace.

9.

PRIORITIZE SELF-CARE.

I have felt the most aligned in my life when I was consciously taking care of myself and putting my needs before other people's urgency. Prioritize self-care as an essential element of your daily life. Enhance all aspects of your health by ensuring ample sleep, consuming healthy meals, and dedicating moments to rest and introspection. This journey won't always be consistent or perfect, but even just having the intention is a good enough start. Be patient with yourself.

NOT SURE
WHO NEEDS
TO HEAR
THIS, BUT ...

You know you're not "behind," right? No one has all the answers or has their life perfectly sorted out, and there's no universal timeline for success or fulfillment. Your life is not a race; it's a unique journey to appreciate. Keep evolving, healing, and growing.

Acceptance is peace.

Hold on to
your softness.

There is so much
happiness in letting go.

Let it end.
Let it change.
Let it hurt.
Let it heal.

Don't let the discomfort of growth trick you into thinking you are regressing.

Never underestimate
how much of a privilege
it is to have access to
your energy. Be mindful
of who and what gets
to experience it.

Interrupt anxiety
with the truth.

Sending love to everyone
finding today to be a little harder.
You are seen, you are loved,
and you are going to be all right.

Put the overthinking to bed
and reclaim your inner peace.
Remember, you don't need to engage
with every single thought you have
(an average of sixty thousand
to eighty thousand daily).
Breathe, relax, let it pass.

I hope you always remember
how many beautiful things
there are about you. You have
so much to offer this world.
Don't deny those things.
Empower yourself with them.

Sending love to everyone who is grieving.
It's disorienting to be in this space,
to feel and hear them everywhere, to
go through periods of being okay and then
experiencing total regression, all while the
rest of the world keeps spinning. Feel
your feelings, and extend grace
and patience to yourself.

The conversation you have with yourself is the most important one you'll have each day. Make it a loving dialogue.

Make peace with what didn't happen.

Mood: Confident Patience. Everything will fall into place exactly as it should, exactly when it should.

It gets better with time.

Let them talk.
Your value isn't defined
by the volume of
their noise.

You've been praised for
your strength and resilience,
but you deserve tenderness.
You are more than your ability
to weather life's storms.

One day you'll look
back and wonder
why you ever
worried.

When you return to yourself,
you set yourself free.

Surrendering doesn't
mean "giving up";
it means letting go
of fruitless struggles
and accepting reality.
Surrendering is a
radical act of self-love.

It becomes easier
to stop taking things
personally when you
realize everyone is
projecting their
own inner world.

Let go of perfectionism.
Let go of material excess.
Let go of the fear of change.
Let go of self-limiting beliefs.
Let go of perceived outcomes.
Let go of energy-draining habits.
Let go of energy-draining people.
Let go of guilt associated with self-care.
Let go of what doesn't nourish your spirit.
Let go of old, negative thought patterns.
Let go of relationships that don't uplift you.

Holding off on celebrating yourself until you're in that place you've been dreaming of is unfair. Appreciate the small wins. Embrace the human experience.

Forgive yourself
every night before
going to sleep.

Have faith that
even better things
are on the way.

You don't have to be "fully healed" to give or receive love, go after that dream, or get to that next level. Healing is a constant state, a lifetime process.

**Let what flows, flow.
Let what wants to go, go.**

Your intuition is the
gift of divine protection.
Trust it more.

Keep healing.
Keep growing.
Keep loving.
Keep going.

Someone's mistreatment of you is
not a reflection of your worth. They are
projecting their past experiences and
traumas, which is their work
to sort out, not yours.

Chapter Two

LOVE.

You are not here to "find love"; you are here to *be* love. Love manifests itself in various forms—self-love, romantic love, platonic love—and yet all grow from a common seed: deliberate, consistent action. Love isn't a passive emotion; it's an active decision that requires commitment. It's not something you just "fall" into as much as it is something you *rise* into by showing up, listening, being present, and putting in the work. It means extending a helping hand to a neighbor in need, offering a comforting embrace to a friend in distress, or simply taking the time to listen to someone's story. Love thrives when it's put into motion.

This becomes even more potent when you realize that at any moment, you're operating from one of two places: fear or love. This widely discussed philosophical and psychological idea explores how these are the two primary colors of the human emotional spectrum. Fear constricts, isolates, and suffocates. Love expands, connects, and liberates.

Think of the countless times fear has subtly steered your actions. It's the hesitation that grips you when you're about to speak your truth. It's the reluctance to let go of grudges and resentment, which is often disguised as self-preservation. It's the self-doubt that whispers discouraging words into your ears, undermining your confidence at every turn. But love? Love is your inner lion. It emboldens you to speak with courage and kindness, to forgive not just others but also yourself, and to trust in your power.

Envision this: you're presented with a life-changing job opportunity in a different city. Fear will cripple you with "what-ifs": What if it doesn't work out? What if I can't make new friends? Love, however, offers a different perspective. It nudges you toward the exhilarating "what-could-be's." It teases you with the thrill of what could go *right,* from personal growth to new connections.

When it comes to romantic love, we've been sold on the idea of fairy-tale endings and knights in shining armor. But remember that choice between fear and love? Real romantic love is built on that same foundation. Fear, in its rawest form, manifests as jealousy and self-doubt—sort of like when you see your partner speaking with someone attractive. This is the fear of inadequacy and loss, deeply rooted in the insecurities and scars of the past. Love, on the other hand, invites trust and open communication, rather than silent resentment or manipulative tactics.

So, forget those age-old tropes. Instead of looking for someone to "save" you, save yourself. Make your love life a living testament to the peace you find in independence, so that when someone does enter your sphere, they're adding to an already beautiful existence, not creating one for you.

Making choices from a place of love not only enhances your own life but also deepens your bonds with others. It means choosing trust over doubt, generosity over scarcity, empathy over judgment. And the beauty of it? This choice is eternally yours to make.

Pause before every decision you make and ask yourself, "Is this rooted in love or fear?" If it's fear, pivot toward love. Choose to have the hard conversation, to take the leap, to trust, and to be vulnerable. When you do this in your relationships, whether it's telling a friend a painful truth for their own good or deciding to be more open with your partner, you deepen your connections in a meaningful way.

This isn't just feel-good philosophy; it's practical wisdom. You can even apply this knowledge when you're faced with social or political issues that ignite different opinions and passionate arguments. Operating from love means taking the time to understand where the other person is coming from. It's about listening rather than just waiting for your turn to defend your stance. It's about seeking common ground and being open instead of doubling down on divisions. Each of these actions transforms not only your own life but also sets into motion a ripple effect, influencing the lives of those around you.

Moreover, love is about boundaries and self-respect. It's not self-sacrificial; it doesn't demand that you deplete yourself for the sake of others. Love teaches you to honor your own needs and to communicate them clearly. It empowers you to say "no" when necessary and "yes" when it feels right, serving as both an external connection and an internal harmony.

So, here's your charge: choose love. It's a radical, transformational act that anchors us to our authentic selves and propels us toward collective well-being. Love is the antidote to divisiveness; it's the key that challenges and heals us. It encourages us to evolve into better, more compassionate human beings.

Remember, every decision you make is a step toward either love or fear. Make it your mission to choose love, consciously and consistently. Your choices don't just shape your journey; they define the type of world you want to live in. And when you commit to love, you're not just existing—you're serving as a beacon, radiating light in a world that desperately needs it. This isn't just your personal revolution; it's the beginning of a global transformation, sparked by one simple yet potent choice: yours.

NINE WAYS TO CHOOSE LOVE.

1.

OWN YOUR UNIQUE BRAND OF WEIRD.

You've got quirks; we all do. Quit hiding them. When you embrace your eccentricities, you not only set yourself free, but you also give others permission to be themselves. Honoring your weirdness invites authentic love into your life. The sustainable kind, where you don't have to keep up some persona you think they'd prefer. That's *real* love, my friend.

2.

TELL FEAR TO TAKE SEVERAL SEATS.

The next time you feel fear creeping up on you, literally call it out. Speak to it out loud, as if it's a guest who's overstayed their welcome at your get-together. Acknowledge its presence, and then tell it to leave. Remember, you're the one driving this life of yours, and love is riding shotgun. Fear can come along for the ride, but it does not have permission to steer, navigate, *or* pick the music.

3.

READ THE ROOM.

When you walk into a room, be it a family gathering, a work meeting, or even your own home, take a moment to gauge the energy. Is it feeding you, or is it draining you? Are you an asset to the space, or are you inadvertently adding toxicity? Love doesn't thrive in toxic environments. Sometimes, the most loving thing you can do is remove yourself from these spaces. That's not cowardice: it's a courageous act of self-preservation.

4.

FOCUS ON WHAT'S IN FRONT OF YOU.

Things you've been through in the past can still hurt today, even if you swear you've healed. Remember, healing is not linear, and it's normal for painful memories to creep up when you least expect them. But try not to get caught up in your past wounds. If you keep picking at your scars, if you keep going back, they will never fully heal. Take what you've learned and carry it with you. Your past has contributed to your present, but it doesn't have to dictate your future.

5.

ROMANTICIZE REALITY, NOT FANTASY.

Movies sell us stories of grand romantic gestures and happily ever afters, but the truth is, real love exists in the mundane. It's how someone looks at you when you wake up with messy hair, or a silence between you and your partner that feels comforting, not awkward. This is the love that lasts—a love based on reality, not on some scripted ideal.

6.

DELETE THE EX-FILES.

Don't keep tabs, don't stalk social media, don't ask friends for updates (and maybe distance yourself from the ones who provide them against your wishes). The relationship ended for a reason. Take whatever lessons you need and grant yourself the permission to let go and move forward with your life, unburdened and refocused.

7.

LET GO OF "WINNING" ARGUMENTS.

If you find yourself constantly needing to win or to be the smartest person in the room, that's fear talking. If you're keeping score in your relationship, nobody's winning. You should be playing for the same team. The end goal of any disagreement should be mutual understanding and growth, not a "win" for your personal scoreboard. Love is not a competition.

8.

PRACTICE
LOVING YOURSELF.

The longest relationship you'll ever have is with yourself. Stop waiting for someone else to give you the love you haven't given yourself. You are not a half waiting to be made whole; you are a full cup waiting to overflow, a complete masterpiece waiting to be appreciated. When you embrace yourself, you set a standard for how others should love you.

9.

TAKE OFF
THE ARMOR.

Being guarded might keep you safe, but it also keeps you isolated. It's hard to experience love—be it platonic, romantic, or self-love—when you're wrapped up in layers of emotional armor. Be brave enough to expose your vulnerabilities; that's where true connection happens. When you take off the armor, you allow love to touch you deeply, heal your wounds, and elevate your spirit. You have endless lovable qualities, and you deserve to be seen.

NOT SURE
WHO NEEDS
TO HEAR
THIS, BUT ...

Love is not enough.
It's about respect.
It's about follow-through.
It's about safety.
It's about value.
It's about honesty.
It's about consideration.
It's about appreciation.
It's about reassurance.
It's about care.

The lack of respect was the closure.
The lack of apology was the closure.
The lack of care was the closure.
The lack of accountability was the closure.
The lack of honesty was the closure.

Change can be scary and exhausting, but nothing is scarier and more exhausting than staying where you know you don't belong.

You will be so happy you waited a little longer for what matches your worth.

If you love yourself, let your actions align with that mindset.

At a certain point, self-respect must outweigh feelings.

The ones who
encourage your
growth and bring
you peace should
get the most time.

Don't let your
empathy impede
your self-respect
or rob people of
experiencing the
consequences of
their actions.

You deserve to be loved.
You deserve to be loved how you want to be loved.
You deserve to be loved how you love.
You deserve to be loved while you are healing.
You deserve to be loved as your authentic self.
You deserve to be loved, flaws and all.

A mature, healthy love is worth being patient for.

Solitude over settling, solitude over toxicity, solitude over misery— any and every day.

Please don't ever abandon yourself again, especially not in the name of trying to be seen, heard, and validated by an unrequited connection. Stop holding on to things that don't demonstrate respect for your value.
You deserve better.

If you want something long-lasting, don't skip the friendship part.

Release what released you.

Stop rewarding inconsistency with loyalty.

I hope you get to experience that soft "I made you a playlist" kind of love. Love that feels nurturing, not traumatizing, ill-timed, or emotionally immature. You deserve it.

A relationship
should complement you,
not complete you.
You complete you.

You deserve people
who are sure about you.

Cherish the
friends who have
secondhand
happiness for you.

It's okay if some
parts of you still
miss what you had
with them, even if it
wasn't perfect. That
doesn't mean they
deserve a spot in
your life again.

Healing.
Trying.
Growing.
Releasing.
Accepting.
Unlearning.
Evolving.

It broke your heart but liberated you from illusions.
It broke your heart but reminded you of your worth.
It broke your heart but affirmed your intuition.
It broke your heart but encouraged your growth.
It broke your heart but ignited your creativity.
It broke your heart but repaired your perspective.
It hurts, but be thankful for the newfound clarity.

You've survived heartbreak after heartbreak, and yet here you are, still honoring your capacity to give and receive love, not allowing those situations to close off the parts of you that make you human. That's brave and beautiful. Protect that.

We romanticize "forever,"
but sometimes the most compelling
love stories are the ones that
teach us how to let go.

You are easy to love.

You become happier
when you realize that
no one belongs to you.
Only you belong to you.
Real love is not possessive;
it's appreciative, respectful
of individuality, and
reciprocal.

Don't expect emotional availability from people who aren't even emotionally available to themselves.

Relationships should uplift you, not drain you.

There's intimacy
in reassurance.

Self-discipline
is self-love.

Not every connection is meant
to end in a committed relationship,
and that is okay. Be more interested
in experiencing life than grasping
onto imaginary outcomes.

Chapter Three

LEARNING, UNLEARNING, RELEARNING.

I want you to take a moment and think about that younger version of yourself from a decade ago. Think about the things you believed in, the fashion statements you made, the music you listened to, the people who influenced you, and the habits you clung to. Really dive deep into the mind of the person you were; think about your fears, your dreams, and your convictions. Hold on to this image for a moment.

Now, reflect on where you stand today and revel in your evolution. Your life has probably changed in ways you couldn't have ever conceptualized, even five years ago. Those friendships you swore would last a lifetime? Well, life happened. Some have deepened, becoming your anchors, while others faded, teaching you the value of impermanence and the beauty of growth. Those once-scary mountains? You've scaled them. The dreams that felt unrealistic? You've either achieved them or replaced them with ones that resonate more with the person you've become. And those boundaries? You've either expanded them or torn them down entirely, redefining your own path.

Along the way, you've undoubtedly faced trauma and challenges, some that tested your very core, but here's the beautiful thing: *you are still here*. None of that broke you. You have transcended every "worst moment" of your life. These experiences molded you, added depth, value, and dimension to your being, even if you couldn't see it at the time. That journey from then to now? That was all the divine workings of learning, unlearning, and relearning.

It's easy to think of growth as a linear path, transitioning from one milestone to the next. But here's the truth: Growth isn't just about moving forward. It's about reflecting, shedding, and renewing. For every new lesson you learn, there's probably an old belief or a misconception that needs to be shed. Embracing this process is how you cultivate wisdom. Growth is as much about what we unlearn as what we absorb anew.

Unlearning isn't always a gentle process. It's a bold act of defiance against everything that's been holding you back. It's the balance between surrendering to the past and embracing the potential of your future. Remember that younger you? Now imagine the older you, the even more evolved you, a decade from now. What stories would you want them to tell? The story of someone who lived a life filled with "what ifs?" or the story of a brave soul who had the audacity to unlearn, rebuild, and continuously evolve?

The process of unlearning requires emotional intelligence, a willingness to embrace vulnerability, and the courage to master your ego. It's a process you can encourage yourself to start right now. Shed the self-doubt and negative self-talk that have held you captive. Release long-held beliefs that no longer align with whom you've grown into or the direction you wish to go in. Throw out the self-sabotaging habits and self-limiting beliefs. Stop shrinking yourself because of societal norms or limiting yourself to the confines of other people's expectations. Free yourself from the weight of preconceived outcomes and lean into the wisdom of acceptance. Recognize the power and grace in changing your perspective.

It's within this unlearning that you find your true self, buried beneath layers of complacency and external influence. The journey does not stop there.

Once you've shed these old layers, the most transformative phase begins: *relearning*. Relearning is the art of making better choices informed by past experiences, new perspectives, and a deeper understanding of yourself and the world around you. It's about refilling your cup with water that is clearer, purer, and more nourishing. It's about giving yourself the freedom to rewrite your life's narrative, one that aligns better with your evolved self.

Maya Angelou, a titan of wisdom and resilience, once said, "Do the best you can until you know better. Then when you know better, do better." This is the essence of relearning. Her life is the greatest testament to it. At just seven years old, following a traumatic experience where speaking out led to the death of the person who caused her trauma, Angelou chose to physically mute her voice, believing that it only brought more harm. For the next five years, her world was void of spoken words.

It was in this era of muteness that Angelou's process of relearning her relationship with language began. While she had lost faith in the spoken word, the written word became her sanctuary. It offered her a safe space where she could explore feelings, ideas, and stories. When she did eventually choose to speak again, it was with an invigorated sense of purpose.

She had relearned the true power and nuance of words, not just as a form of communication, but as tools for healing, advocacy, empowerment, and transformation. Her writings became a blueprint for others navigating their own journeys of learning, unlearning, and relearning. Her journey from a mute child to one of history's most profound authors and speakers underscores the incredible capacity we all have for stepping into new versions of ourselves and reveals how, sometimes, like how the sun sets to let the moon shine, it takes a step backward to truly leap forward. In the face of trauma, with a little bit of consistency, discipline, and unwavering belief, you, too, can rediscover and reinvent yourself with newfound purpose.

Remember, in this world that thrives off conformity, be brave enough to unlearn and audacious enough to relearn. Stay committed to this process, and you'll find yourself growing in ways you hadn't imagined. Stay curious, stay resilient, and, most importantly, trust the process. Because every twist, turn, and transformation brings you closer to the most authentic version of yourself. Embrace it. Celebrate it.

NINE THINGS
TO UNLEARN.

1.

BINARY THINKING.

Life isn't an on-and-off light switch. Life thrives in the spaces between. Unlearn rigid black-and-white thinking and embrace nuance and complexity. It's about recognizing that everything in life isn't confined to two extremes. By stepping out of a "this or that" mindset, you open yourself up to a world of possibility and new information; you embrace a spectrum of identities, experiences, and perspectives. You elevate your consciousness. Expand your mindset, embrace complexity, and witness your understanding deepen.

2.

INSTANT VALIDATION.

We're so used to living in a world of instant feedback that most of us aren't even conscious that we are hooked on immediate gratification. Social media companies design their platforms and algorithms like addicting casino games. The engagement, the likes, the DMs affirming your selfies, the idea of having followers—all of this is meant to hijack your brain's reward system and keep you hooked. But true self-worth isn't about how many likes or comments you get; it's about valuing your authentic self and loving that individual wholly, despite occasional feelings of self-doubt. So do your best to unlearn the need for immediate praise and learn to separate your self-worth from external factors. Make it a discipline. Let your actions be driven by passion and integrity, not the desire for someone else's approval.

3.

PERFECTIONISM.

Perfection is a myth. True growth is birthed from missteps, embracing vulnerability, and daring to step out of your comfort zone. Lean into every facet of your journey, acknowledging that every flaw, every imperfection, is a stepping stone to becoming the best version of yourself. Seek excellence, not perfection, from your best level of effort and awareness, and allow yourself the grace to learn and evolve.

4.

COMPARISON AS A BENCHMARK.

Seeing someone else's light does not mean you are in their shadow. Know that there is room for everyone to shine. You can be both happy for others and remain rooted in your own narrative. Instead of gauging your progress against theirs, center your own progress and use only your past self as the benchmark. Let your individual experiences, challenges, and triumphs be the compass that guides you, not the fleeting paths of those around you. Their story is not your story.

5.

THE FEAR OF SAYING "NO."

In your quest to fit in, people-please, or avoid conflict, you've probably found yourself silencing your true desires or thoughts, hesitating to assert that simple yet powerful word: "No." But every "no" voiced is a step closer to a "yes" that genuinely resonates with you. Finding the strength to decline is not a rejection of others; it's an affirmation of your own boundaries. Unlearn the urge to always agree and realize that prioritizing your needs is a healthy way to respect yourself and others.

6.

SUPPRESSING EMOTIONS.

Bottling up your emotions is akin to shaking a soda can and leaving it in the freezer; it's only a matter of time before it explodes. Subscribing to the idea that suppressing your vulnerability is a sign of strength is the ultimate self-sabotage. Real strength? It's not in silent suffering or wearing different masks. It's in tearing down the façade and having the courage to say, "I feel this. This is my truth, and it is valid." It's in confronting, not concealing. So, let your authentic expression breathe. Allow yourself to experience the growth and connections that arise from honoring your emotions. Unlearn emotional restraint, and remember that your emotions don't make you weak; they make you human. Your emotions are the most honest reflection of your inner world. Don't suppress or judge them. Embrace them, learn from them, and let them guide you toward a state of balance.

7.

AVOIDANCE
OF FAILURE.

Don't let fear paralyze your progress. By shying away from risks, you diminish your capacity to grow. Without failure, you miss the chance to truly push and expand your limits. You also miss out on the opportunity to sharpen your strengths, illuminate your purpose, and understand yourself more vividly. Unlearn the fear of failure and let each misstep become a path toward newfound wisdom.

8.

RESISTANCE
TO CHANGE.

Change is a call to transcend, not a cue to retreat. It is the universe's way of saying, "I love you too much to let you stay the same." The solace of the familiar, the safety you feel within your comfort zone, is often the very cage that stunts your growth. You can't stay there forever. To unlearn this resistance is to free yourself. Be open to and step into the vastness of what you can become. Stop holding yourself back. You deserve more than that.

9.

BEING QUICK
TO JUDGE.

Immediate judgment overlooks nuances, potentially damages relationships, slows your growth, and perpetuates societal stereotypes. To combat
this, it's essential to get into the practice of pausing before drawing con-
clusions, interrogating your assumptions, and seeking deeper, more informed understanding. By choosing empathy over judgment and curiosity
over quick categorization, we cultivate a more compassionate, balanced,
and open-minded approach to life.

NOT SURE
WHO NEEDS
TO HEAR
THIS, BUT ...

Time doesn't heal all wounds.
The work you do does.

Anger is a secondary emotion to what you're actually feeling.

You can't change people, but you can change your proximity, reactions, and boundaries.

Short-term discomfort is necessary for long-term growth.

The secret to getting unstuck is radically accepting where you're at now, with grace. Let go of expecting perfection from yourself. You won't always be your most productive, make the best decisions, or get it right. A little self-compassion will take you a long way.

Sending love to anyone reckoning
with their own toxic habits and trying
their best to unlearn them. You are seen,
you are brave, and with a little bit of
discipline, you are going to make it.

Believe people's actions.

Healing starts with
accepting the truth.

Your guilt for setting a boundary
and choosing your peace
will fade. Trust.

You are allowed to put yourself first.
You are allowed to take up space.
You are allowed to eat.
You are allowed to outgrow people.
You are allowed to say no.
You are allowed to change course.
You are allowed to rest.
You are allowed to walk away.
You are allowed to take your time.
You are allowed to have periods of stagnancy.
You are allowed to be proud of yourself.
You are allowed to start over.
You are allowed to change your mind.
You are allowed to cry it out.
You are allowed to take up space.
You are allowed to speak up.
You are allowed to change.
You are allowed to love yourself.

Never regret choosing to be
a good person. Everything comes
back full circle, and a pure heart
will always have the last word.

Growth requires vulnerability.
Growth requires accountability.
Growth requires willingness.
Growth requires exploration.
Growth requires release.
Growth requires space.
Growth requires discipline.

The first person you
need to be loyal
to is yourself.

When you know
in your heart that
you deserve better,
don't ignore that.
Go get it.

You are not
responsible for
weathering every
storm alone because
you "don't want to
bother anybody."
Ask for help, love.

Stop comparing.
Everyone's growth
has its own rhythm.

Use your power to empower others.

You can find intimacy in learning to enjoy your own company.

There is no past version of yourself that you "need to get back to." Life is about flowing forward and growing with the new lessons learned.

You have to take responsibility for your progress. The savior you're looking for is yourself.

You are forever changing; just make sure it's for the better.

Every time you put
yourself out there,
despite the possibility
of rejection, you validate
your courage and willingness
to take risks. Embrace
rejection as a form of
empowerment.
Your journey is one
of hope, not self-shame.

No matter how pure your heart or how right your actions, someone will always find fault. Choose joy. Don't let others' contagious negativity dictate your journey.

Practice saying exactly what you mean.

Act.
Even if fear
is present.

Improving over
impressing.

Be intentional with your heart.
Be intentional with your words.
Be intentional with your thoughts.
Be intentional with your time.
Be intentional with your energy.
Be intentional with your life.

It's time to get clear about what you want.
It's time to get clear about what you need.
It's time to get clear about what you value.
It's time to get clear about what you deserve.

The way you
speak to yourself
can change your
entire world.

Remember,
you're still healing.
Give yourself grace.

Be proud of your growth.
This version of you has
a lot less tolerance for
the things you used to
accept, and that is
a beautiful thing.

Chapter Four

CREATIVITY.

Dear Creatives,

Your perspective is so important. You turn ambiguity into clarity, translating the language of the soul into something we can see, touch, hear, and feel. Artists, you are the emotional architects of society—materializing human experiences, creating spaces that offer us refuge, elevating our consciousness, and making this puzzlingly, beautiful thing called life more bearable.

Your talent? That's not just your asset, it's your responsibility—to yourself and to a world that deserves the imprint only *your* voice can provide. Nurture your talent like you would a garden; water it with discipline, fertilize it with broad, sought-out experiences, and prune it with the ability to receive constructive critique.

In those inevitable moments when doubt creeps in, when you question the worth of your art, your voice, or your vision, remember this: you're in excellent company. Every master started as a novice. Every icon began their journey with just an idea and a glimmer of hope. Every forest began as a single seed.

Take my story, for example. In 2009, I was just a fifteen-year-old kid in North Carolina with a clunky laptop, a strong will, and a love of art in all its forms. With a shoestring budget—just enough to snag a domain name—I took to Tumblr and launched WE THE URBAN. At the time, it was a far departure from the WE THE URBAN we know today. I posted on a wide range of subjects, spanning high fashion, music, contemporary art, cutting-edge design, and technology. I was churning out content at a relentless pace, curating ten to fifteen posts daily. This was at a time when social media wasn't the omnipresent force that it is today; it was still an emerging space, full of untapped potential, undiscovered niches, and uncharted territory waiting to be explored.

By the time I was sixteen years old, when the Tumblr staff noticed my work, the word "influencer" hadn't even entered the popular lexicon yet. The concept of a "fashion blogger" was still so novel it ruffled feathers among the fashion elite. This became apparent when Tumblr invited me to New York Fashion Week, where having bloggers in the room at any runway show was deemed taboo. Despite their hesitation, this was a trip that didn't just shift my trajectory, it shattered the glass ceiling of what I believed was possible for myself. Suddenly, everything I'd hoped for wasn't just a pipe dream; I saw a future where I could etch out an entire existence fueled by expressing myself creatively on the internet.

Maybe I was naïve, maybe it was a positive by-product of the hypomania I was experiencing (and had no name for until I was twenty-one), or perhaps it was a helping of delusion and audacity, but I genuinely believed I could build something transformative. As my following grew, so did my ambition. The blog wasn't enough; I wanted to give people something tangible, something they could hold, get inspired by, and appreciate. That's when the idea of a magazine crystallized. Armed with big creative ideas, a ton of research, and a relentless drive, I went from a teenager posting aesthetically pleasing content on Tumblr to one of the youngest editors in chief in the world. The blog eventually became the first Tumblr–turned–print magazine and one of the most followed pages on the platform. I was a kid in the South, commissioning fashion shoots and taking business meetings in school bathrooms between (and during) classes, juggling the dual roles of a student and a burgeoning entrepreneur. This life I'd manifested earned me the nickname "The Teen Anna Wintour" in press clippings. I got to present on national TV with Kelly Rowland, host shows on Pharrell's i am OTHER network, produce *WE THE URBAN Magazine* release parties at New York Fashion Week, employ my creative friends, and travel the country.

But even the brightest stars can fade. Tumblr's eventual decline taught me a harsh lesson: the importance of ownership. When you don't create something inherently yours—something immune to the rise and fall of social media trends—your relevance ebbs and flows with the digital tide.

My dreamlike rise morphed into stagnancy and depression. The community I'd spent thousands of hours growing migrated to other platforms, "friends" faded, funds evaporated, the phone stopped ringing, and that creative fire that used to fuel entire issues of magazines? Gone. All while I was in the throes of navigating the constant existential crisis known as your early twenties.

Self-doubt wasn't just sliding into my DMs, it set up shop in my psyche. *Did I lose my creative spark? Will I ever find it again? Was it all a fluke? Are my ideas even any good?* I couldn't see it at the time, but this period of doubt became the most important tool in my story.

If there's one constant in the creative journey, it's uncertainty—the kind that gnaws at your spirit and tempts you to abandon ship. At some point, you have to pick yourself up and make the conscious decision to let uncertainty become your friend. Realize that although it fluctuates, your creativity is always there. Deciding to move forward in a healthy way is one of the highest creative acts.

Creativity isn't just confined to painters, musicians, or writers; it's an essential part of everyone's psychological makeup. It exists in the mother who conjures a meal from pantry odds and ends, in the entrepreneur who sees promise where others only see pitfalls, and in the teacher who knows just the right metaphor to turn confusion into clarity. It's in how you approach daily life, navigate complex conversations, solve problems on the fly, or curate a playlist.

We limit ourselves when we categorize creativity as a trait only found in traditional artists. We overlook the profound ways in which our unique creative energies can influence not just art galleries or concert halls, but boardrooms, homes, futures, and hearts.

After Tumblr, I transmuted all that doubt into curiosity and shifted WE THE URBAN to Instagram. I reimagined our content strategy to embrace all the unique, visually captivating elements that defined the brand. But I also introduced a fresh perspective—grounded in emotional intelligence and sociopolitical awareness—that was both uplifting and deeply personal. In doing so, something beautiful happened.

When I leaned into the purest expression of myself and pushed through the resistance to restarting, I opened up a pathway for my creative dreams to come true.

When you engage with the world from a place of authenticity, you stop wasting energy trying to fit into molds that were never meant for you. Your true self becomes your greatest asset, and you start to attract opportunities, relationships, and experiences that align with your core values and ambitions.

During the initial COVID-19 lockdown in March 2020, I honed my writing as an outlet for my emotions and a platform to support others. Driven by the empath in me, I leveraged all my newfound extra time to offer solace to those in pain. The messages struck a chord, resonating with millions of people and creating a meaningful impact in the world. Embracing the full arc of the creative journey, with all its ups and downs, uncertainties, and revelations, is a deeply rewarding experience.

It's normal to question the worth of your creations or your place in the world. But the more you face your doubts head-on, the more you will understand your unique value. Find refuge and purpose through the fog of uncertainty.

Whether you identify as an artist or simply a human with something to say, sow your seeds. Nurture them, believe in them, even when no one else does. Because who knows? It could very well grow into a forest that provides shade, solace, and inspiration to a world that didn't even know it was waiting for you.

NINE WAYS TO UNLEASH YOUR CREATIVITY.

1.

MAKE ROOM FOR BOREDOM.

In a world obsessed with productivity and constant stimulation, boredom has gained a bad reputation. Yet, boredom is the blank canvas on which creativity paints. Allow yourself to get bored occasionally. It's in these moments of stillness that the imagination wanders, providing you with unexpected and groundbreaking ideas.

2.

TRUST YOUR INTUITION.

There's a reason it's called the "creative instinct." Creativity often means trusting your gut feelings, even when they defy logic or popular opinion. Learn to cultivate this internal compass, as it often guides you toward creative gold.

3.

TAKE RISKS.

Creativity thrives on uncertainty. When you're too comfortable, you're less likely to explore new territories or challenge the status quo. Whether you're experimenting with a new medium, taking on a project that feels a little out of your depth, or simply opting for an unconventional solution, risk-taking is a crucial component in the recipe for creativity.

4.

CAPTURE IDEAS RELENTLESSLY.

Creativity often visits unexpectedly. When an idea lights up your mind, don't let it vanish into the ether. Write it down, sketch it out, voice-record it—capture it by any means necessary. Review these ideas regularly; you never know which one may blossom into your next big project.

5.

COLLABORATE.

Two heads are often better than one, and the combination of different perspectives can result in extraordinary outcomes. Don't hoard your creativity. Share your thoughts and ideas with trusted friends or collaborators and be open to their feedback and suggestions. The result could be pure magic.

6.

EMBRACE VULNERABILITY.

Putting your creative work out into the world can be daunting, but don't let fear hold you back. Embrace the vulnerability that comes with sharing your ideas. Whether it's met with praise or critique, the act of revealing your creativity itself is a success and a path to growth.

7.

SEEK INSPIRATION.

Creativity doesn't exist in a vacuum. Surround yourself with people, places, and things that inspire you. Attend art exhibits, listen to music, or delve into books and articles that spark your curiosity. By regularly immersing yourself in stimulating environments, you're more likely to stumble upon creative inspiration.

8.

CELEBRATE
SMALL WINS.

Creativity is often a long game, requiring patience and persistence. Celebrate your small wins along the way—each completed chapter, each artwork sold, each well-received social media post. These moments of victory keep you motivated and remind you that you're making progress, even if it doesn't always feel like it.

9.

CREATE FOR THE JOY OF IT.

Sometimes the pressure to produce something great can be overwhelming. Remember that the core of creativity lies in the joy of the process itself. When you focus on the intrinsic pleasure of creating, you're more likely to stumble upon unique and impactful ideas.

**NOT SURE
WHO NEEDS
TO HEAR
THIS, BUT ...**

You are never "too old" to start again.
You are never "too old" to follow your dreams.
You are never "too old" to switch directions.
You are never "too old" to learn something new.

**Being authentic is
more important than
being popular.**

You deserve to think highly of yourself.

Don't let social media turn you into a carbon copy of what you see working for others. Be yourself.

Visualize it.
Speak it.
Write it down.
Work on it.

Mindset matters. Routine matters. Consistency matters.

Balance.
Patience.
Consistency.

If you're constantly
waiting for "the right time,"
you'll be waiting forever.
Allow yourself to begin.

Turn it into art.

Be consistent with your words.
Be consistent with your work.
Be consistent with your goals.
Be consistent with yourself.

Stop letting fear govern your life.
Stop letting fear get in the way of your dreams.
Stop letting fear keep you stagnant.
Stop letting fear block you from new chapters.
Stop letting fear dictate your every move.

Practice being happy for others. There's room for all of us.

Take. More. Chances.

Don't give up
on the person
you want to
become.

Dare to desire more
than what you believe
you deserve.

You are good enough.
You always have been.

Don't play small.
Acknowledge your growth.
Appreciate your wins.
Practice acceptance.
Be proud of yourself.
Hype yourself up.
Celebrate yourself.

Please keep creating your art,
no matter how many people see it.

Never underestimate
the healing power of
a good playlist.

It starts with
believing you can.

When you honor
your creativity,
you invite your
truest self to
the table.

Your ideas matter
and deserve to
be realized.

Begin where you are; use what you have.

Focus on yourself.
Focus on loving yourself.
Focus on your happiness.
Focus on your goals.
Focus on practicing presence.
Focus on being at peace with who you are.

You still have time.
Time to iron out that idea.
Time to set those boundaries.
Time to ideate about that project.
Time to transform.
Time to accomplish your goals.
Time to finalize and fine-tune.
Time to do the right thing.
Time to choose your own path.
Time to let go of the past.
Time to heal in solitude.
Time to assess and rearrange.
Time to figure out who you are.
Time to change your mind.
Time to learn, unlearn, and relearn.
Time to be a better you.
Time to find healthy love.
Time to work on your craft.
Time to embrace the human experience.

It's always been you vs. you.

Risk is your ally.

May you have the
discernment and
courage to remove
yourself from spaces
that drain your energy
and cloud your vision.

Chapter Five

WELL-BEING.

"Health is wealth." It's one of those age-old sayings we've all heard before. But in today's world of extreme hustle culture—and extreme rest culture—it seems we're all a bit lost on how to truly embody this mantra. We find ourselves oscillating between extremes: we grind until we're burnt out, then retreat into prolonged rest without being able to find the sweet spot in between. Feeling trapped in this perpetual cycle can be disheartening; running faster isn't always the answer, especially if you're headed in the wrong direction, and perpetual solitude can very well turn into stagnation.

Beneath the surface of this continuous motion lies fundamental truths awaiting your recognition: You were not designed for mediocrity. You are not going to feel stuck forever. Your existence is not just about surviving; it's about thriving. It's about living up to every ounce of potential embedded in your DNA in the healthiest way possible. However, to tap into this well of potential, you must first prioritize your well-being.

Though self-care activities have their place, overall well-being isn't just splurging on a spa day, working out one time, or going on an annual retreat. Well-being is about the daily, conscious decisions you make to honor the totality of your being. It's telling your body, "I've got you," and recognizing that your mind, your emotions, your spirit, and your energy are not just parts of you; they *are* you.

Reaching optimal well-being requires self-protection. Every time you ignore your emotional, mental, or physical health, every time you push past your boundaries without regard for your own peace, you do yourself a disservice. And here's a hard truth: the world will take everything you give and still ask for more. So, your task? Knowing where to draw your line in the sand. Define your boundaries and then, come hell or high water, stand by them.

You can't treat your home Wi-Fi signal better than your own well-being. You wouldn't stand for dead zones in your living room or slow speeds in your bedroom. Just like you ensure seamless wireless connectivity throughout your space, ensure consistent well-being in your life.

Daily practices lay the foundation for well-being. Start with the simple habits: a few minutes of mindfulness in the morning and at night, a short daily walk outdoors, or a handful of water breaks throughout the day. Big transformations often stem from modest beginnings. This is about building sustainable habits by repeating small acts of self-love over an extended period of time, not achieving brief highs.

In your journey to find good equilibrium, don't just chase happiness. Chase *wholeness*. Happiness is fleeting. Wholeness, on the other hand, means accepting every part of yourself: the beauty, the light, and the shadows. When you embrace this holistic view of well-being, and when you put action behind it, happiness becomes a natural, accessible state, not something you'll ever need to force.

And your body—a miraculous temple worthy of your love in every state—also deserves your intentional care. Every meal you consume, every ask you say yes to, every single choice you make, is an opportunity to honor it. This isn't about vanity or perfection. It's about respect, gratitude, and love for the vessel that carries you through this life.

This isn't an all-or-nothing sprint. It's okay to move at your own pace. Listen to your body, tune into your mind, and respond to your soul's nudges. Every step, no matter how small, is still a step forward. Celebrate those victories and thank any missteps for the wisdom they gift you.

Let this collection of quotes serve as both a mirror and a beacon. Reflect on your choices, understand their impact, and be guided toward a future where well-being isn't just an aspiration but a lived reality. Embrace the journey, with all its challenges and triumphs, and remember: you're equipped, empowered, and deserving of a life that radiates well-being in every facet.

NINE WAYS TO BOOST YOUR WELL-BEING.

1.

GET ACTIVE.

When you reframe your perspective to see exercise as an activity you enjoy rather than a daunting obligation, you unlock every holistic reward. The physical benefits are a beautiful consequence, but the beauty of movement shines through its impact on your mental health and soul. It creates harmony, ignites a sense of accomplishment, increases confidence and productivity, and cultivates a deep appreciation for the incredible vessel that carries you through every experience.

2.

DON'T QUIT. REST.

Giving yourself space to recharge is crucial to sustaining success and well-being. It's okay to take a step back when things get overwhelming, but don't give up altogether. Reevaluate and adjust your pace if needed, but always keep going.

3.

CHERISH YOUR COMMUNITY.

Humans are social creatures, and genuine human interaction is irreplaceable, even in our digital age. A part of boosting your emotional and mental well-being requires nurturing meaningful connections with friends, family, and the community you have in your life. You don't have to handle everything by yourself, and you don't have to be at rock bottom to seek out support.

4.

SEEK LAUGHTER.

Laughter is the best medicine; let it be your daily free therapy. Its infectious energy is the universal symbol of happiness. It cuts through stress, elevates our spirits, and strengthens our immune system. Make it your business to consciously pursue moments of humor, be it through a shared joke, a comedy special, or funny memories. As you do so, remember that every single chuckle contributes to your well-being.

5.

GET QUALITY SLEEP.

Sleep is an elixir for the mind and body. You just can't function at your best when you're not getting enough rest. Sleep is the time when we plug into our own source of energy, just like we recharge our devices. And it goes beyond rest; sleep plays a role in mood regulation and your overall cognitive function. When you're in deep slumber, your body repairs, regenerates, and rejuvenates. Meanwhile, your mind sifts through the day's experiences, cementing memories and processing emotions. Embrace a quality sleep routine, see it as a self-care ritual, and experience the positive impact it has on your well-being.

6.

SAY NO. DO IT OFTEN.

In our quest to please others and be available, we sometimes forget the importance of setting boundaries. Boundaries are not barriers, but rather markers of self-care and top-tier respect for yourself and others. Recognize when to say no, ensure time for yourself, and prioritize your well-being. It's these types of healthy boundaries that create spaces where you can thrive. As you continue to cultivate the art of discernment, remember that every *no* paves the way for a more meaningful *yes*.

7.

REDISCOVER ANALOG.

In a world where our days are spent staring at screens, there's an unmatched sense of grounding in reconnecting with analog pleasures. Whether you're doodling on paper, painting, whipping out a board game, or simply enjoying the sensation of turning a book's pages, it's these moments that will ground you and counterbalance digital overload and its negative effects on your overall well-being. Prioritize these moments daily.

8.

DANCE IN YOUR LIVING ROOM.

You don't need a reason, a partner, or even music. Sometimes, the most soothing thing for your well-being is to dance like nobody's watching, right in the middle of your living space. It's joy, exercise, and therapy, all rolled into one. There's no one there to judge your moves or critique your rhythm. It's just you—fully present in the moment, in deep connection with yourself—releasing pent-up emotions, rejuvenating your spirit, and stimulating your body.

9.

BREATHE.
HYDRATE.
REPEAT.

Breathing deeply and intentionally calms the nervous system, centers the mind, and reenergizes the body. Hydration, meanwhile, nourishes every cell of your body, laying the groundwork for optimal function and rejuvenation. Both acts serve as continual reminders of the basics we often overlook in our bustling lives. Return to these foundational practices, fostering a sense of balance in your well-being journey, so you can navigate the complexities of life with clarity.

NOT SURE
WHO NEEDS
TO HEAR
THIS, BUT ...

Do at least one nice thing for yourself every day.

Keep your empathy,
but protect your energy.

Burnout is not
a badge of honor.
Rest is productive, too.

I'm proud of you
for trying.

Your body is worthy of your love, in every stage, in every state.

If you have a therapist, tell them the truth. You are not there to impress them; you are there to receive genuine support.

Meditate.
Journal.
Hydrate.
Stretch.
Repeat.

Keep taking care of yourself,
even when you're tired.

Dear People Pleasers,

You are not responsible for everyone
else's happiness. You don't have to pretend
you're happy, sacrificing your well-being for the
sake of others' needs. Adulthood has taught me that
sometimes you just have to disappoint people.

Your mental health comes before everything.

You are enough.
You always have been.

Wherever you are in life,
I hope you're experiencing joy,
taking it easy on yourself,
and finding peace through the
turbulence. You deserve it.

Be selective with
your focus.

Sending love to
everyone experiencing
the worst of their
mental health lately.
I'm proud of you for
doing your best to
be okay. The journey
hasn't been perfect, but
you made it. And you
will continue to.

Seasonal depression
is not exclusive to fall
and winter. Wishing
peace and comfort to
those going through
the motions and trying
their best. Be patient
with yourself.

Chin up, there's no
need to grieve the
person you could've
been. You're still
breathing, so you still
have time. Keep going,
keep evolving.

You deserve a life that feels good for your nervous system.

Every new chapter of your life demands a different version of you.

Prioritize
morning silence.
That invaluable
time dedicated to
centering your spirit
is the compass
for your day.

Always do what's
best for your well-being,
even if it means embracing
a season of solitude.

Intention must be
powered with action.

Sending love to those
feeling disconnected
lately. Feeling lost
is a sign of growth.
Embrace this chance
to rediscover yourself.

You are resilient.
You are capable.
You are loved.
You are beautiful.
You are enough.
You are talented.
You are chosen.
You are worthy.
You are inspiring.
You are smart.
You are needed.

Have you been hydrating?

It's really important for you to recognize and honor your worth right now. Prioritize your cup.

Exercise shouldn't be a chore; it should be a celebration of your body's abilities and the benefits they bring to your mind.

Every day,
notice something you
love about yourself.
Write it down.

Stop saying yes
to things that
drain you.

Chapter Six

AFFIRMATIONS.

Never underestimate the power of your words. The language that you choose to use, both internally and externally, doesn't just describe your reality; it creates it. Affirmations are not only statements; they are announcements to the universe that you are open, willing, and ready for the changes you've been looking for. It's the practice of being present in deciding your life's narrative.

Science backs this, too. We see this happen with the placebo effect. Research in neuroscience has shown that when people take a placebo, believing that it will be an effective medication, their brains can produce happy chemicals like endorphins, which naturally alleviate pain. A 2014 study published in *Science Translational Medicine* proved that the brain actually activated the same neural pathways when participants took both a placebo and an actual pain medication. Affirming relief creates a real, biological response. Your body hears everything your mind says. Words can calm our nervous systems, stabilize our heart rates, and help us sleep.

The nocebo effect, which is the opposite of the placebo effect, is worth mentioning as well. This is when negative expectations can make the outcome much worse. The nocebo effect also influences pain management. A study published in *PAIN* in 2017 showed that patients who were told to expect high levels of pain during a medical procedure experienced significantly more pain than those who were given neutral information. What we affirm to ourselves and others doesn't only have the power to heal, but also to harm.

We also see the power of affirmations demonstrated throughout the history of humanity. Many cultures and spiritual traditions around the world have long recognized the power of affirmations. In ancient rituals, chanting and spoken affirmations were believed to bring healing, protection, and manifestation. Though our environments have changed in the present day, the message remains the same: the words we choose carry a life-changing frequency.

You boost your power when you start recognizing this force in your daily life. Every day, you're surrounded by an overwhelming amount of stimulation, information, and opinions. Scrolling through hundreds of thousands of posts on social media in a month, watching movies, listening to music, and even having casual conversations can play a huge role in shaping your thoughts. But what if you were to consciously filter and select the affirmations you expose yourself to? Practice discernment and allow yourself a chance to experience true clarity and peace.

If you keep believing you're bound to fail, your brain inadvertently perceives everything as reinforcing that belief. When you continually affirm that you are capable, your brain starts to recognize opportunities to prove that right. It's not about blind positivity; it's about conscious recalibration. It's recognizing when a script no longer serves you and having the courage to rewrite it. It's understanding that every day presents a new chance to show up more authentically.

The link between emotions and affirmations cannot be overstated. When you combine your affirmations with genuine emotion, whether it's love, excitement, or gratitude, it amplifies their potency. An affirmation fueled by feeling resonates on a different level. It's not just about saying, "I am confident"; it's about repeating it until you actually *feel* that surge of confidence in every fiber of your being.

Affirmations are not magic spells. They don't always work instantaneously, and they are not a substitute for action. You can't just affirm "I am wealthy" while lounging on your couch all day. Similarly, affirming "I am successful" won't lead to success without dedication, strategy, and consistency. The vision requires actions that align. The more you lean into the art of practice, the more you realize it will always be the combination of belief and effort that creates tangible results.

Affirmations, like our lives, are complex and ever evolving. What was true yesterday might not be as true today. As you grow, learn, and experience, your needs and desires will naturally shift, and that's okay. Don't be so rigid. Allow your affirmations to be adaptable. Let them align with where you are currently; let them guide you.

With each affirmation, be precise. Be passionate. But most importantly, be persistent. Revisit and refine them regularly. Don't let missteps or temporary roadblocks deter you from your aspirations. Throughout this journey, yes, you will have moments of doubt, but you can choose to see them as reminders to dig even deeper and reaffirm your commitment. Remember that each word you utter, each phrase you repeat to yourself, isn't just a string of syllables—it's a declaration of intent. It's a pact between you and the universe, a promise to yourself. Hold on to these words; let them be your anchor when you feel lost. Keep them close to your heart; let them be the catalysts that propel you into a reality where dreams aren't just spoken but lived.

NINE WAYS TO ACTUALIZE AFFIRMATIONS.

1.

WRITE THEM DOWN.

The act of writing your affirmations down gives them a tangible form. Using a dedicated journal can amplify this effect, turning the journal into a sacred space for your goals and aspirations. Over time, this journal can serve as a reflection of your growth, allowing you to revisit and reaffirm your commitments.

2.

SAY THEM ALOUD.

Your voice has power, and speaking out loud involves bravery. It's one thing to think or write privately, but vocalizing your beliefs and intentions is a vulnerable experience. It's in this vulnerability that the magic often happens. Your entire body will always listen, feel, and align with the intent behind the words.

3.

VISUALIZE THEM.

As you repeat your affirmations, conjure a vivid mental image of what your life would look like if the affirmations were actualized. Take the story of Jim Carrey. In the '90s, struggling to make ends meet, he wrote himself a check for ten million dollars for "acting services rendered," dated five years into the future. He visualized, affirmed, and believed in this check's value. In 1994, just before his self-set deadline, he received a movie role in *Dumb and Dumber* that paid him the exact amount. This wasn't magic; it was the power of affirmations at work, backed by dedication and belief.

4.

BACK THEM UP
WITH ACTION.

The daily practice of affirmations gradually shapes your subconscious mind, aligning it more and more with your conscious intentions. Don't just state your intentions; back them up with tangible steps that bring you closer to your goals. A vision without a plan is just a dream.

5.

EMBRACE REPETITION.

Ever found yourself humming a song after hearing it just once? That's the power of repetition, and affirmations work similarly. The more we recite and believe in them, the more they root themselves in our psyche, transforming into our core beliefs. Repeat your affirmations daily and watch what happens.

6.

PERSONALIZE THEM.

It's essential to keep in mind that for affirmations to be effective, they must resonate with your inner truth. Repeating statements that you don't believe will likely not yield the outcomes you desire. Authenticity is key, which is why personalized affirmations that speak to your unique experience and aspirations are often the most impactful.

7.

CHALLENGE YOURSELF.

Put this to the test. Start with a seven-day affirmation challenge. Select one affirmation each day, write it down, and repeat it to yourself during moments of reflection. Monitor the changes in your attitude, interactions, and overall mood. More often than not, you'll find yourself more aligned with the opportunities that resonate with your affirmations.

8.

SHIFT YOUR PERSPECTIVE.

When you're creating affirmations, it's crucial to frame them in the present tense. Instead of saying, "I will be confident," assert, "I am confident." This tiny shift can have profound effects. This approach keeps them within reach, pushing you to act on them *today* rather than "someday."

9.

LOOK AT YOURSELF.

Consider the daily ritual of looking into the mirror. For a lot of people, this routine goes beyond checking physical appearance. It's a moment of reflection, of silent dialogue with oneself. The thoughts during these moments can be pivotal. Affirming, "I am beautiful, inside and out," can influence how you carry yourself throughout the day.

NOT SURE
WHO NEEDS
TO HEAR
THIS, BUT ...

My allegiance is to my peace of mind.

Say it with me:

One thing about me,
I always get through it.

My mind is focused.
My heart is pure.
My soul is at ease.
I am ready to receive.

When I speak
with intent,
my body
listens.

**Grief is a path to healing;
I allow myself to feel and heal.**

Replace FOMO with JOMO
(Joy of Missing Out).

Replace "I should've known"
with "Now I know better."

Replace "What will they think?"
with "What do I think?"

Replace "I'll be rejected" with
"I'll be directed."

Replace "They're so far ahead"
with "Their path isn't mine."

Replace "I'm too old" with
"Experience is on my side."

My peace is non-negotiable.
I've overcome a lot, and
I refuse to compromise
my inner tranquility for
anyone ever again.

I trust my journey,
even when the
path is unclear.

Everything I go through, I get through and grow through.

I trust that I am
not missing out on
anything while I am
busy upgrading myself
and my standards.

I am at peace with all that I cannot control.

Say it with me:

I love myself through transition and discomfort.
I love myself through the times I stumble.
I love myself through my mental health episodes.
I love myself through times of loss and grief.
I love myself through every stage of growth.

Who cares how they perceive me? I'm the one who has to live with me, day in and day out. As long as I know myself, I know peace.

May this season be one of change, clarity, humility, and happiness.

If I never try, I'll never know.

I am easy to love.

**Everything is going to be okay.
Everything is going to work out.**

I am not afraid to be seen.
I do not have to hide myself.
I am worthy of occupying space.
I do not have to dim my light.
I am authentically me, and that is my strength.

Everything meant for
me is within
my reach.

I am doing the best
I can with what I have,
and that is enough.

What is for me will always
find me, as long as I am
making choices that put me
in its path.

I am only interested in peace
and progress. Anything that
gets in the way has to go.

Dear Self,

You'll find peace when you
lean into uncertainty as a form of
empowerment. Remember, life's not
just about tolerating unpredictability,
but mastering the art of thriving
within it. Uncertainty is your stage,
not your cage. You got this.

Everything does not have to
be perfect for me to start.
My progress does not
require perfect
conditions.

I am more than enough.
I am more than good enough.
I am more than talented enough.
I am more than capable enough.

My sensitivity is my superpower.

Their mistreatment of me
is not a reflection of my
worth. It's the echo of their
own unhealed past, which
is their work to untangle,
not my burden to bear.

What I focus on, I become.

Say it with me:

Everything isn't worth my energy.
My peace is more important.
I am not worthless.
My self-worth is inherent.
All my efforts will be rewarded.
I refuse to give up on myself.
I am deserving of good things.
I deserve love that feels safe.
Sadness doesn't last forever.
I combat stress with self-compassion.
I am going to be just fine.

Repeat after me:

I'm going to be okay.
If it costs my peace, it has to go.
Everything isn't worth my energy.
I will not give up on myself.
My peace is more important.
I deserve the very best.
Sadness won't last forever.
My self-worth is inherent.
My efforts are not in vain.
This too shall pass.

ACKNOWLEDGMENTS

Writing this book has been an extraordinary journey, one I couldn't have embarked on without a constellation of stars guiding me along the way.

To my aunt Debbie, thank you for being a beacon of light and inspiring me to keep shining from the very beginning. To my parents, Willie and Adeira, your legacy of boldness and your sacrifices for our beautiful childhood have shaped my very being, and I am eternally grateful for them. Letisha and Alex, my siblings and first best friends, your laughter and support have been pillars of my existence.

My deepest gratitude extends to my grandmother Mattie Greene, a southern Black woman who was strong-willed and kindhearted, for exemplifying pure love, calling me a star, and recognizing my power before even I could.

To Hannah, Elyse, Eileen, Dante, and every other soulmate connection I've fostered along this journey, your friendships heal my inner child, inspire my creativity, and give me the fortitude to keep going, to keep creating, and to keep believing in myself. Thank you for affirming me. To Marissa Shrum, founder of Remember, I Love You and one of the first believers in WE THE URBAN, thank you for your generously brave investments in my vision, your love, and your counsel. And to every collaborator and person who has believed in me, thank you from the deepest wells of my heart.

I have to give a thank you to the struggles—the challenges, stillness, lows, and highs—that have shaped the way I process life. This journey has enabled me to offer solace to myself and others, turning all of my lows into collective healing.

Thank you to this beautiful community of readers and supporters of WE THE URBAN, those who have been here since the beginning, and those new to our shared journey. Your thirst for healing and inspiration propels me to show up and raise the bar continually.

In every word and on every page, I see the imprints of all the souls that have touched mine. This book is not just my story, but a reflection of all these incredible people and experiences that have shaped me—thank you for being part of this unforgettable ride.

Published in the United States by Clarkson Potter/Publishers, an imprint of the Crown Publishing Group, a division of Penguin Random House LLC, New York. ClarksonPotter.com

CLARKSON POTTER is a trademark and POTTER with colophon is a registered trademark of Penguin Random House LLC.

ISBN 978-0-593-79620-7
Ebook ISBN 978-0-593-79621-4

Printed in China

Editor: Sahara Clement
Art director: Ian Dingman
Production editor: Terry Deal
Production editorial assistant: Taylor Teague
Production manager: Jessica Heim
Compositors: Merri Ann Morrell, Nick Patton, and Hannah Hunt
Copy editor: Rebecca Zaharia
Proofreader: Mindy Fichter
Marketer: Monica Stanton

10 9 8 7 6 5 4 3 2 1

First Edition